W. S. K.

My Adirondack Pipe

Memories of a Pleasant Month Spent in the Adirondacks

W. S. K.

My Adirondack Pipe
Memories of a Pleasant Month Spent in the Adirondacks

ISBN/EAN: 9783337180638

Printed in Europe, USA, Canada, Australia, Japan

Cover: Foto ©ninafisch / pixelio.de

More available books at **www.hansebooks.com**

My Adirondack Pipe.

Memories of a pleasant month spent in the Adirondacks, by

W. S. K.

Printed for Private Circulation.

PRESS OF
WILLIAM R. JENKINS,
PUBLISHER, BOOKSELLER AND STATIONER,
850 SIXTH AVENUE,
NEW YORK.

My Adirondack Pipe.

I

IT is a harmless indulgence, that hurts nobody, and gives me much pleasure; so I stick to it. Heretofore, when I have returned from the Adirondacks, much as I loved my pipe in the woods, I have found on my return to the city, that my dislike of the pipe, and preference for a cigar, returned as well. Not so this year. I smoke my cigar in the daytime, but when evening comes, I now look forward to my pipe, with the keenest pleasure.

It is quite an ordinary affair. A briar wood pipe, pretty well colored, the amber mouth piece almost worn through; but about it circle many pleasant memories, of the past summer.

And when I sit in my easy chair, with my feet perched up high, the taste of my Adirondack pipe on my lips and its fragrance filling my nostrils, I feel my blood run faster, my eyes brighten, my senses dilate, my whole being pulsate, as when I stand under the broad blue sky, of the beloved Adirondack woods.

The smoke from its bowl rises faster and thicker, and as its clouds encircle my head, the pictures gradually fade from the walls of my room, the light changes, and I see once more before me, the scenes of my first day in the mountains.

Oh! the glorious ride on the stage top, that perfect September day! Through the cool crisp air of the early morning, and then, after breakfast, on through the pure bracing atmosphere, gradually mellowing and warming, as the sun rises higher in an almost cloudless sky.

On! On! all day with three or four merry companions on the top, discussing every subject under the sun, from Wagner's music to opera bouffe, from bird shooting to hunting hippopotami, from Henry George's theory to the latest cut in tennis.

Then we meet the outgoing stage, crowded with young men and women all looking hale and hearty, and well browned by the sun.

A "Where have you been" as we recognize a friend, and the coach is past.

Then comes the attendant baggage wagon, loaded up high with enormous trunks, containing the costumes and war paint, in which the young people have been masquerading, for so many weeks, and also, many trophies of the campaign, no doubt.

Later, the tedium of the trip, is relieved by a broken strap or two, or a lost horse-shoe and—here we are at Blue Mountain Lake.

Then on again, after dinner, through the woods for ten or twelve miles. The road is bad, and conversation flags; sometimes we get down and walk a piece.

Now the road is better and our speed increased; we pass a hunter out with his dog, evidently after birds, and—there is Long Lake in the evening sun.

The road follows a ridge along the eastern shore, and three miles down the lake, in sight of a church, which marks Long Lake village, turns abruptly to the left, and plunges into a pine grove. All these scenes pass rapidly before my eyes, under the helpful veil of the smoke; but now I hear a rattle and a roar, and with a dash we go down a heavy loose plank road, and the house appears in sight at the right.

To the left down a sharp decline, is the tennis court. There is no one playing—but under the surrounding trees, several girls are lolling in a hammock, and young men are grouped around on the ground, some with rackets, evidently resting from the game.

There is a shout and and a yell, and then I see my brother jump to his feet, and run to meet me, as the stage draws up at the door.

Handshaking and greetings. He relieves me of my traps and we enter the house.

Numerous faces peer curiously at the new comer, their costumes looking odd to the eye of one accustomed to the conventional dress of the city, and I remember one in particular, in a black and white striped flannel dress and swagger cap to match, that reminded me for all the world, of a Prussian guard house, with a pretty face peering out of it.

A large barn of a hall, with an office, decorated with a large moose head on one side; a rack filled with hats, wraps, books and rackets, on another side, and doors on all sides, are the first sights that greet a new arrival.

There is no one in attendance, but a soiled specimen of a man, collarless, in cardigan jacket and slippers, with dissipated eyes, a shaggy head of hair, and a long moustache, dyed black, and showing brown at the roots. This is Walter. Jack of all trades he runs the office, fetches water, carries wood and is deputy sheriff.

When appealed to by my brother in regard to my room, he is not sure whether I can have No. 15, although he promised it, only half an hour before. My brother insisting, he leads us up one flight, and opens the first room, at the head of the stairs.

I am surprised to find it well furnished and clean. And as it also has a beautiful view to the north, I cut short all argument, by installing myself.

II

YES, I think I'll fill her up again. My pipe is not a large one, and the tobacco is not strong. It's a light mixture that I have smoked for many years, in fact as long as I have been going to the Adirondacks. I find it does not burn the tongue, the odor is delicious, and its chief charm to me is the smoke.

Watch its wonderful greys and blues, and see how gracefully it curls and wreaths.

Just so was I smoking, idly puffing at my pipe, lying full length, flat on my back, in the afternoon sun, gazing up at the stationary clouds overhead, when a recruiting party came my way, and a voice startled me with :

"It is almost four o'clock, and if we want to mount the Pinnacle to see the sunset, it is time we were off."

There is much talking back and forth, followed by a shoving out of boats, shipping of oars, and arranging of seats; but all is ready at last, and all are paired off satisfactorily, or, at any rate, if any one is not satisfied, he or she dare not show it.

Lazily, we row down the lake, for we are in no hurry,—sometimes side by side, to pass a jest or point out some beauty in the landscape, sometimes stringing out in a procession ; now rowing hard to pass one another and then paddling hand over hand to rest, or await some straggler.

Down the lake, as down the early

years of life, rowing is a pastime, as existence is a pleasure.

All are evidently full of health and spirit, enjoying the air they breathe, the company they are in, and their surroundings, but all unconsciously—the essence of true pleasure.

Thus we drift down to the woodpile, a landmark on the lake, from which starts the road we wish to take. It is a wide wagon road at first—but divided into groups, and, engrossed in conversation, we do not notice our surroundings much.

And such groups! Pretty girls in mountain dresses, of all colors· and combinations, that show off effectively against the green background of the woods,—the men, some in shooting coats, knee breeches and stalking caps, others in tennis suits and striped caps, look as picturesque as men ever can look.

We have a half hour's stiff climb before us, and so walk slowly, pulling grasses or picking a flower as we go, which often serves as a pretty excuse for a couple to lag behind. And eyes can say so much, while a field flower is being given and taken.

We pass several small houses belonging to natives and stop at one to take a drink of spring water. The old man, who kindly brings us a glass, cannot help beaming, as he sees all the bright youthful faces about him, and delivers himself of some sentiments, as to the advantages of being young, and adds some compliments to the ladies.

The party now divide, the restless ones, seeking for some novelty, think they can make a short cut, and take across fences. The more sober remnant pursue the path, more lenghty but more sure, that winds up to the top of the Pinnacle.

Unnecessary to add that the would-be time savers, arrive there some ten minutes after the rest of the party.

And now we are on the rocky top of the Pinnacle, with the country gloriously spread at our feet

It is a calm beautiful evening, with not a cloud in the western sky, where the sun, growing more crimson each minute, is slowly nearing the horizon.

Immediately under it, reflecting the shadowy sides of Owl's Head, lies Clear Pond, beautifully peaceful, embedded in the green woods, and evidently at some elevation above Long Lake, which stretches like a broad winding river, as far as the eye can see from south to north. Its mirrorlike surface is only broken by the many islands that rise from its bosom, and here and there by a boat, that looks insignificant in its size and motion.

In the east, myriads of small grey clouds, already tinted by the broken rays of the setting sun, float in the sky, and below them broadens a vast panorama of valleys and enchaining mountains.

To the north and nearest to us, is Mount Kempshel; next in order and in majesty are Mt. Everett and Santanoni; in the distance towers Mt. Seward, and on the horizon, forming a chain of pale azure peaks are Ampersand, Marcy and McIntyre.

The densely wooded mountains to the east, are growing purple in the evening haze, as though the trees had assumed that hue, while at our feet and west of us, the hills are ablaze with sensuous reds and yellows, running over all, from shore to peak, from ridge to ridge. It is the most glorious mingling of myriads of shades of blood red, carmine and crimson, of ochre, yellow and green, that nature ever presented to a favored eye.

All this we drink in, as this beauty or that, is pointed out by one or another, as this color or that—this light or that shadow—this cloud or that island claims the attention.

Our voices hushed, no sound is heard, but the recurring note of the cowbell, or the last whistle of a bird, mellowed by distance.

It is growing late—the sun's fiery disc just touches the line of the mountain ridge, poises there for an instant, then rapidly sinks behind it.

We all watch it intently and silently, as it grows less and less, until, now, there is only a faint edge of vivid light to be seen.

Again it hangs for an instant motionless, then suddenly disappears.

Somehow we all feel saddened, and it takes us some time to recover our voices.

The air grows chill at once, as though the earth suddenly realized how long it will be, ere she will again see the sun's cheerful face, and feel his warming influence.

In strange contrast with the purple mountain sides, and the black shadows that are already beginning to fall, the mountain tops and the floating clouds, burst into a glow of soft rosy light. They vie with each other in their efforts to recall to the earth, in beautiful and glowing colors, the memory of the sun that is set.

So might some dear friends of one that is departed, uphold his best thoughts, reflect them to the world, and cherish his memory.

Inclination bids us stay—'tis the most beautiful time of day—this half hour after sunset, but the wiser ones of the party urge a prompt start for home.

Coats are all buttoned, the pairing process gone through with again, and the start made, with many a lingering backward glance.

Progress is slow, at first, the ground is rocky, and full of holes, overgrown by long grasses and low bushes, forming pitfalls dangerous to the ankles; but after this tract is passed, and the path reached, we make a dash down hill, single file, at a terrific rate, and it is wonderful to see the girls run.

Stop! there is a fence and bars! don't take them down! let us climb to the top and jump down on the other side!

So! up you go! now, steady! give me your hand and jump! Bravo! another, and another—then, on we go. What a delightful sense of exhilaration and freedom, from the rapid motion of the scamper down the hill.

Now we cross a field;—yonder is a flock of sheep; how they look at us sideways, and eye us with curiosity, until suddenly, one takes alarm at some word or motion, and runs,—then all drive after, helter skelter, like a whirwind, and amid the thumping noise of many feet on the sod, they are off to the furthest corner of the field.

Another fence—another opportunity to touch soft hands; and one with a laugh, and another with a scream over they go, and we are on the main road again.

Then a girl race, for a hundred yards or so—how they fly—and as they pass a cottage, a dog leaps out barking at every jump, and jumping at every bark.

He cannot understand what all this noise is about, why all these faces are bright and all these voices fresh and ringing; for looking into the cottage you see only drawn sallow sober faces, their wearers appearing prematurely aged, and showing in their bearing as in their features, how severe is their struggle with nature, to wrest from her a mere subsistence.

It is milking time; and now we pass two or three docile cows, dappled buff

MY ADIRONDACK PIPE.   21

and white, with soft melting eyes, and short horns. A man is milking. "Good evening to you," as we pass.

A yoke of fine heavy oxen, of a dark dun color, lie lazily in our road, chewing their cud, and greet us with a half menacing, half fearful gaze.

They raise their shoulders heavily, from the ground, as if about to rise, but as they see we pass without molesting them, they fall back into their lazy, restful positions, their large eyes following us, until we are out of sight.

For a few rods, we now traverse the woods, already grown dark, and emerge on the lake, at the woodpile.

Who shall go into whose boat, being decided, and the arrangement of wraps being concluded, we start to row homeward.

The younger members of the party,

eager to be home first, or to show their prowess at the oar, dash off at great pace.

The older ones, only too glad to lengthen these delicious moments, pull a long, slow, steady stroke, loathe to break the smooth surface of the water, which stretches from shore to shore, like polished steel, reflecting the western bank in deep black shadows.

There is not a breath of wind; the stars are coming out, one by one, in a grey blue sky, that has lost its radiance, but is soft and pearly.

Round Island rises gigantic over our stern, as though suspended high above the waters of the lake.

Slowly we approach the bridge, regretting every stroke that bring us nearer home. We pass familiar points and bays, but they look so different by this dim light, we hardly know them for the same.

Under the bridge. There is the moon, a slight slim silver crescent in the west, hanging within easy reach of the tree tops; a fit ornament for Diana's chaste brow.

A rowing song floats on the still air, and falls in with the cadence of the rising and sinking oars. Then as we catch sight of the lights of our house, the song changes to one, suggestive of a wanderer's return home.

Our boat grates on the sand—and tired, but with a contented and peaceful feeling about our hearts, we jump ashore, in the failing light.

III

COME old pipe, the day's duties are done, and thou and I, may now enjoy another of those pleasant hours in close communion, hand in hand and lip to lip.

Thou art growing old and worn, but age only adds to thy beauty, in my eyes. Age has deepened and mellowed the complexion of thy face, but brought no furrow to thy brow.

Not weaker, but stronger dost thou grow, but thy strength is sweet to me. Thou art slow to make friends, but the fires of thy heart being once kindled, and thy friend tried and proved worthy, thou dost become his complement.

Dear old friend! thy exterior may look cold and polished, but thy heart is warm, and in the right place. Though in our hours of communion, thou pourest forth column after column, and volume upon volume, yet art thou discreet as the moon. Ever ready to solace in time of trouble, weariness or sadness, ready to sigh at my sorrow, or chuckle at my jest, thou shalt be in future, as in the past, dear to my heart, and the sharer of my inmost thoughts.

Speak now to me of the sights and sounds I love so well! Speak of the woods and the fields, of the sky and the water!

No?—Why does the smoke hang like a sheet above my head? It neither rises nor falls, but floats heavily in the air, like a thick veil.

What makes the day so dark, is it mist or smoke?

See, the sun answers your question. Observe how high he is, and how red, as he vainly struggles to break through the opaque atmosphere.

Mist would have been dispelled ere this, drawn up by the powerful arms of the rainmaker, into the semblance of white fluffy clouds flecking a blue sky.

But now the sky is hidden, and the sun already halfway to the zenith, looks a small dull red ball, in the murky atmosphere, like the moon on a hot summer's night.

Only a small portion of the lake is visible, and the moutains look far off and blue. It is certainly smoke, probably from some distant forest fires

How they must burn and what acres of trees must fall victims to the fiery tongues to produce the smoke, which covers us like a cloud, at such a distance from the scene of the disaster.

There is no wind to carry off the smoke, but the air is cool and bracing. It is not a day to invite us either to the woods or to the lake, and many turn to their books, or to letter writing. But we have still other resources.

"It is a gem of a day for Tennis, and I challenge you to a set of singles!"

"You" is a trim figure in a pleated skirt of some light colored material, short, dark blue, tight fitting, small pocketed, and high collared coat, and a blue and white, striped, swagger cap, surmounting an abundance of fair hair.

"You" has bright eyes, of the speaking kind, that possess the most delightful downward and upward motions imaginable, not to mention a bewitching sidelong glance, that only comes into play, on special occasions, but speaks volumes. Their color is immaterial, I do not know that I could tell, whether they are blue or grey, but I can recall their speech distinctly.

Her mouth brackets small teeth, and her nose, well,—even prejudiced as I am, I must confess, that it is red—but only from exposure—only because she is not afraid of wind or sun, and I have no doubt that in a ball-room in mid-winter, it looks as fair as the rest of her complexion.

"You's" name is Harriet, but every one calls her Harry; not that she is at all masculine, but it is a family way of abbreviating names, and I like it.

My challange being accepted, I fetch the rackets and balls, then down the slope we tear, to the tennis court, near the lake shore.

"I give you choice of court and service."

"No? you will not have service; then call!" Up goes the racket, twirling in the air, and ere it falls flat, Harry calls "Rough."

"Rough it is, and yours the first service."

Harry takes the balls, and assumes her position at the outer line of the court, ready to serve.

Is she not a picture as she stands there, bending slightly forward and downward, and sends the ball, with a horizontal stroke of the racket, swiftly over the net, scarcely three inches above it?

But that is nothing; wait till you see her run.

Game follows game; sometimes Harry has the advantage, sometimes I, until we have both warmed up to the fun, and, as I win my service, "five all" she cries, and adds, "Now, if I can only win this game."

As "this game" will decide the set, we commence it in a very determined way, both eager to win.

You can see how carefully she serves, for fear of making a "double."

Here comes the ball—and I return it, badly—almost to her racket,—back it comes to me, and this time I put it to the other side of the field,—now see her run—she is there before the ball, quick as a man, graceful as a woman, and with just the least little jump, she takes the ball, and returns it diagonally across the field, as far from me as possible—with a great effort I reach it, raise it and drop it—just over the net—she makes a brave dash for it, but cannot reach it in time.

That is what a woman calls a mean trick.

Thus it goes on rally after rally, volley after volley, amid the sound of that lingo, that grows musical to the lover of the game.

Fifteen-love,—thirty-love,—'Vantage in,—Game!

What matters it who wins the game or who the set? It's not that I play for, I know.

But the life out doors—with the sod beneath, the sky above, and the woods around you.

The pleasure of living, of running, of jumping, of leaping, of falling, if you will; the pleasure of feeling the blood, coursing through your veins, at a rate that brooks no coat on your back, or cap on your brow, of swinging the racket at arm's length, and placing the ball at will,

The pleasure of sound—in the musical language of the game, the excited shout of a ball well returned, or an adversary foiled; the merry laughter that naturally follows the incidents of the game; and the enthusiastic "bravos" or "played" of the interested on-lookers.

The pleasure of sight—of men in picturesque costumes, with hat drawn over the eyes, or cap hastily thrown to the ground, the right sleeve rolled up, and arm bared to the elbow, their young and well developed figures, undisguised by awkward garments, in full and graceful play; of women simply dressed, strong and well, complexion clear but browned, eyes bright and flashing, standing firm, and straight as an arrow, with lips parted and nostrils dilated, or running across the field, with the speed and grace of a fawn.

The pleasure of the contest—the eager struggle, as the tables are turned again and again. The training of all the senses to the command of the will, when, for the nonce, all depends upon oneself and upon one play.

The excitement and suspense of dence—'vantage in — dence—'vantage out—and back again.

All these I say, are pleasures, which far outweigh the mere sense of victory ; they are far greater and more permanent ; they create brain and sinew— and make Tennis a royal game.

IV

J HAVE just disposed my rod and gun, old friends too, upon the walls of my room, where they will hang probably, for another year; that long year which must elapse, ere I can again use them.

No more groceries and blankets to put up, no boats to be loaded; no rowing down the lake before others are astir; no more crossing of carries with the dog straining at his chain, a gun on your shoulder, and a pack on your back, underfoot sometimes muddy and slippery, but the woods overhead always beautiful; no more camp life, no sleeping in the open air on balsam boughs, no more hasty toilet making in the morning, while ones hands are almost freezing ; no flap jacks and maple syrup for breakfast; no putting out of dogs, while the mist still hangs low over the lakes ; no returning to camp in the dusk, with the spoils of the day; no more fishing at sunset ; no more camp fires and ten o'clock toddy in the evening nor snoring at night !

No—not for another year.

But there's my pipe ! Behold I had almost forgotten thee, old friend !

Come to my aid ! Dispel my vain regrets ! Pour forth thy fragrance, and wreathe thy charmed circles, and who shall say, that these things are not as sweet in the remembering, as in the doing.

Blessed be memory, and blessed be tobacco ! Memory that registers, and tobacco that revivifies these scenes.

For as the power of heat brings forth the words that have been written with vanishing ink, so the aroma of tobacco, renews the pictures, once traced upon the tablet of memory,—and as I inhale its fragrance, and lean back in my chair, I am once more seated in the stern of my boat, with gun across my knees, and the guide is pulling our craft, heavily laden with camp kit and supplies, out of the slang, choked with lily pads, into the bright rippling waters of Round Pond.

It is the glorious afternoon of a day that promised but poorly. We have rowed eight miles down Long Lake, and crossed the carry with our boats and loads, since we started, in the early, cold, raw and misty morning. Now, the sun is shining brightly enough, the deep blue sky, and a few white wind clouds, are reflected in the water, save near the shore, where the mountains change the hue, and trace their image on the lake's surface.

To our right as we enter the pond, is mighty Everett, looking far more impressive than from Long Lake, with its triple crown, and great spurs, diverging to Belden Pond and Catlin Lake.

Before us, is Santanoni, a worthy rival, towering apparently quite as high, and with a long waving sky line.

Both mountains are well covered with hard wood timber, which is beginning to change under the influence of the crisp frosty nights; only here and there a tongue of dark green, shoots along the top of a ridge, or boldly into a mass of wonderous bright colors, showing where some accident of soil, or destruction of first growth has given the resinous woods, a foothold.

To our left, on the contrary, the low hills are covered by soft wood trees, and cedar, pine, and spruce, balsam, hemlock and tamarack, mingle their various and varied shades of green.

Happily the lumberman, and the fire have spared this pretty pond as yet, and its shores are wooded to the water's edge. It could not have looked more beautiful, or more peaceful, when the eyes of the white man first saw it, than it does this day, as our two boats float side by side, skirting its shores, in search of a suitable place to build our camp.

We finally turn into North Bay, and land on a sandy beach near the mouth of a brook. Mindful of the wild character of the lake and not wishing to detract from the unbroken appearance of its shores, we pitch our camp, a little way back in the woods, where no passing eye could possibly detect it.

Then follow the pleasures of pitching camp.—Selecting a good place for the dogs, and a level spot for the tent, cutting and setting the poles, driving the pins, and adjusting the canvass.—

Then a good back-log must be found, and in building a new altar, a living tree is generally sacrificed. In an incredibly short time the fire is made and lighted, and one of the guides goes in search of tender balsam boughs for bedding, while the other unpacks the baskets, and, after clearing a path to the brook, prepares supper.

Soon the first returns, bending under his green fragrant load, skilfully adjusted on a withe. The bed is made, the blankets unstrapped and spread, and by that time, the sun having set, and darkness fallen, while we were engrossed about our work, supper is declared ready.

After supper, pipes,—every body smokes,—and then huge four-foot logs are piled upon the fire, and the flames swirl up in great sheets, higher than our tent, amid the snapping and crackling of the burning bark, and the hissing of the fresh sap, oozing from the ends.

Great showers of sparks pursue each other in endless numbers, whirling and circling with the smoke, darting swiftly upward, impelled by the great heat, and disappear high overhead, amid the leaves of the surrounding trees.

Stand with me, your back to the fire, and look out into the dark woods that surround us. Notice how peculiar the colors of the leaves feel : you do not recognize the greens and yellows of daylight. How strong and sharp the shadows, and how they change and move, as the flames flare and veer with every current of air.

Look up, and see the white smooth bark of the birch, the glossy shining trunk of the beech, and the knarled surface of the maple tree, as they tower overhead like huge spectres ; see their leaves, how they tremble, and twist, and twirl, stirred by the powerful upward current from our camp fire. And above and beyond all, the black dome of the night, studded with bright stars, twinkling merrily, in this cold air.

Think you, having seen all this, you can ever forget it ?

Fill your eyes and ears with the sights and sounds of the camp at night, and then roll your blanket about you, and turn in.

Next morning we rise at daybreak. The fire is lighted and breakfast prepared, while we are making our morning ablutions.

After breakfast, the morning being fine, we start on our hunt.

My brother and his guide go to Catlin Lake, a one mile portage, and they have to carry their boat and rifle.

I land my guide with two dogs, in East Bay, and return to my watch ground.—

Here am I all alone, on a point terminating North Bay, with boat drawn up, and rifle at my side. I expect it will be an all day affair, so make myself comfortable—find a good seat, shaded from the sun, commanding the lake, then light my pipe, and gaze contentedly over the waters.

These watches are long and sometimes tedious, but any one fond of outdoor life, can find enough to amuse and interest him.

The first impression is one of silence and repose, the day is fine and warm, rich in yellow sunshine, and mellow breezes, that but slightly stir the lake's surface, and faintly rustle in the tree tops.

There are no song birds left; only two or three little yellow birds, no larger than a sparrow, sometimes hover about, with a chirp not unlike that of their city confrères; or the startling hammer-hammer of the woodpecker suddenly breaks upon the stillness.

Or you are roused from a revery, by the shrill cry and rushing wings of a brace of ducks as they pass by with a swoop.

Or, more rarely still, the ear is pierced by the sound of a trumpet note high overhead, which attracts the eye to a line of black dots, faintly visible, against the blue vaulted sky; straight and true as a line of soldiers, and like them, marshaled by a single leader—a flock of wild geese, on their rapid journey southward.

Or an eagle suddenly appears, circling high above some conically peaked ridge. You never notice him approaching, but are first aware of his presence, when you see him, as now, majestically floating, in those magnificent curves that he sustains to a circle, by one or two strokes of his mighty wings. Round and round he goes, tireless; then back again, until the vision swims,—finally, without an effort, without any apparent volition, the curve of his flight changes, with a graceful S like sweep, and he disappears over a ridge.

Or you leap from your seat, at the sound of splashing water, only to see where a kingfisher emerges wet and dripping, bearing his glittering burden, swiftly and silently along the surface of the lake.

Or a hawk crosses the azure arena, chased by a screaming mob of rowdy crows and pert yellow birds, crying thief, and actively harassing their victim from all sides, as he quickly wings out of sight.

The water adds its quota of stirring life in jumping fish that flash for a second in the air, looking several times larger than they really are, then fall back into the lake, making wide circles that ripple up to the shore.

On land there is but little life, and I

can remember but one instance, when on my watch ground, I have seen a fox, and at another time a hare.

The sun has not been standing still, but has freed itself from the intervening pines, and is pouring down upon my head, scorching face and hands. The glare of the sunlight on the water, is very trying to the eyes, and after a prolonged and searching gaze over the lake, the sight of the green woods affords rest and relief.

Little puffs of wind emerge from every western indentation of the shore, and streak the lake like ribbons fluttering towards you, breaking the rays of the sun, and making to westward. a white dazzling sheet; to the east the waters lie cool, unruffled, deeper in hue, and rich with shadows.

How many times a day does the body

thrill, at sight of a rock or stump, momentarily transformed by some trick of light or shade, into semblance of a swimming deer; how many times does the heart beat fast, at the sound of a dog's melodious voice, bursting from the opposite ridge!

But to-day, the first rifle that cracks in hearing, is on the farthest shores of the pond. It is four o'clock, and I know it must be the call of my returning guide. He has made a half circuit of the lake, following the comb of the ridge, and after travelling many miles, has emerged at the outlet.

I row to fetch him—the dogs are with him, and he has shot two partridges in the woods.

We slowly row home, stopping frequently, the guide resting on his oars, and expatiating on the distance he has travelled, the tracks he has seen, the trouble this or that dog gave him, and his judgment, as to where the deer he started, have run to ; all, interpolated, frequently, by commands to one of the dogs to lie down. Major is dead tired from the run, and asleep with his nose between his paws; but Sport, restless and disobedient, insists on sitting up and sniffing the air.

Soon after our return to camp, my brother and his guide come in, also without any venison. They report, they have seen and heard nothing of the game all day.

Not much game certainly, but the day has been fruitful of memories.

" I am tired of crossing these logs on the way up to camp; let us take the axes, and clear the path of these fallen trees, while the boys are getting supper." "At it then, one at each end!" "Swing the axe, and bury its head!" Haak—hak—haak, hak—for an hour—through the dusk, and into the darkness.

And oh how soft and grateful, feel the balsam boughs, as after our labor, we stretch at full length upon the ground, watching with glistening eyes, the partridges broiling before the fire, in company with juicy slices of English bacon.

Next day, we wake to find it raining, slowly and steadily, with heavy mists on mountains and lake,—an all day rain.

We spend our time putting camp to rights; driving in a nail here, or chopping away a limb there, arranging our cooking stores, and making things generally, as comfortable as possible.

Then, after the guides have built a

roaring fire, that will last several hours, we read aloud from books and magazines, that we have brought with us. The boys take most delight in stories that deal of hunting antelope and buffalo and grizzly in the far West; but frequently interrupt the reading, by their quaint remarks and commentaries, and by their desire to see the pictures.

In the afternoon, more reading, then cleaning of guns, putting together of fishing rods, and adjusting of reel and line.

By five o'clock, as we had anticipated, the rain stops, though there are still no signs of clearing. So encased in rubber coats, my guide and I, resolve to try our luck fishing.

I use a light fly rod; but I know there are no trout in the pond, and can only look for perch, or bass, and intend to fish with worm bait. For this purpose, we had brought along a supply of worms, in a pepper box, and to keep them fresh, we had placed it at the root of a ttee, and covered it with a handful of soil. Now—when I open the box, I find to my astonishment, that there are only two or three worms left in the soil which filled the box. The rest have evidently made their escape, through the minute holes in the lid

However, those that are left suffice to catch some small fish, that in turn serve for bait.

The air is cold and raw, the clouds grey and leaden, and low, and it is gradually growing dark. We are rapidly getting chilled, and catching nothing but small fish—perch, bass and bullheads.

But we stick to it, and finally find a hole, where I strike a good sized fish. My rod bends double, and for a few minutes the fish makes things lively, as he dashes this way and that; sometimes splurging at the water's surface, sometimes sulking, and sinking down as far as the line will let him.

Finally tired out, I land him, a good pound and a half perch. Quite as beautiful as a trout, I think, as I look at his bright red fins, laid flat upon the shining scales of silver and gold.

In a few minutes I strike and land another, almost as large.

With this we are satisfied, and row home in the dark, guessing at the general direction, until we are close enough to see the camp fire through the trees.

We land, so thoroughly chilled that our teeth chatter—but are welcomed home to a big roaring fire for the outer man, and a searching drink of whiskey, for the inner.

After that—a fish supper—no lemons and no fish knives.

The following day we hunt on the Mt. Everett side of the pond. My brother again kindly takes Catlin Lake, as he has his guide to carry the boat. My man takes the dogs up one of the spurs of Mt. Everett, and leaves me as before on Round Pond. This time, however, I watch on a small island, near the outlet, about a hundred yards from shore.

The day has opened dark and dreary. with flying clouds and now then a slight sprinkling of rain, so that a rubber coat is very comfortable

As the sun mounts higher, the low clouds disappear, but the wind still holding in the south, other clouds, large and white and massive-looking, mount from the horizon, and swiftly scudding across the sky, are frequently precipitated to the earth, while the laughing sun looks on.

I do not dare to build a fire, for the wind is blowing right from me, in the direction of the runway, and for the same reason, I do not smoke. So I am fairly miserable.

But the dogs are running in hearing all day, and many a time, as the voice of one or the other rings out, growing louder and louder every instant, approaching nearer and nearer at every bound, do I expect momentarily to see a deer leap in.

Off goes my rubber coat; a hasty examination of the gun, and then how I scan every nook of the shore, and every foot of the water between me and it.

And many plans to cut off the deer in this or that contingency flash through my brain.

What if a deer came and skulked; or if he swam, and cutting off that little bay, gained the opposite shore, before I could reach him, or get into range.

Of course, in such a case, the imaginary deer, was always a buck, and carried a magnificent pair of horns; and of course, the guides would quietly listen to my story, but would never believe, but what if they had been there, they could have gotten the deer.

But no! the dog has taken a turn and is making a long swing back around a ridge; now his voice grows rapidly fainter, until I can no longer be certain, amid the blowing of the wind, whether

I still hear the dog's voice, or the echo of my imagination.

Slowly and reluctantly, I lay down my gun, and again don my rubber coat.

Not once, but three or four times during the day is this enacted, and in these moments of expectation and excitement, when the eyes are bent to catch a sight of the game, and the ears are strained, not to lose a warning note of the chase, lies the chief charm of deer hunting. About three o'clock, when I have almost given up the hunt, and with a dog audible in the distance, I hear the splash which means, a deer in the lake.

There he is—above the outlet—a buck—and swimming towards me, but fortunately heading into the wind, so that he will probably not scent me. If he keeps on his course, as he is, he will pass the island, about midway between it, and shore.

Impatiently I wait, keeping out of sight, until he arrives at that position, then,—my coat is off in a trice, and I creep down the back of the island, gun in hand, to my boat.,

Noiselessly the gun must be laid on the seat, noiselessly I must shove off and—embark, no easy task, when the oars are amidship, with no place to rest them.

This successfully accomplished, I paddle around the end of the island, that brings me behind the deer. Now he is in sight, and I bend to the oars, throwing all the strength and power I possess into every stroke, taking great care, not to splash the water, in placing the oars, and in taking them out.

I know the general direction, and never

look around, but pull, pull, pull—with all my might. The boat bounds forward at a great rate, and the noise of the water foaming and dividing at the bow, and swirling at her sides, from the violent action of the oars, is soon caught by the sharp ears of the swimming buck, and I get notice of the fact, by hearing him plunge, as he accelerates his pace

As I look around, I cannot help remarking his speed, which is simply marvellous, when the slight legs that he uses are considered, and speaks for the tremendous power of his muscles. Another thing I learn by looking around is, that as the deer has somewhat changed his course, I have rowed considerably out of my way.

Correcting my course, I now gain on him, as with all his strength, he is no match for the boat, and I soon have him cut off, committing, however, the common error, of overreaching my mark, and slipping by the deer.

I drop my oars and pick up my Winchester.

How my hands tremble, and my whole body quivers from the exertion of rowing.

My lungs go like a pair of bellows, and the air escapes from them, in sobs; my gun seems a terrible weight, and the barrel, dreadfully top-heavy.

With one glance at the nearing boat, the buck, turning off sharply at right angles, in his course, lifts himself bodily out of the water, in his mighty plunges forward. The water flies in all directions, and the white foam boils around him; then he settles down to his work again, and only his head and neck are visible.

Bang! goes my gun.

Again the buck fairly bounds forward, as though his feet touched bottom, but he keeps on,—his head erect,—and rapidly increases the space between us.

I have now the choice of taking to my oars again, to cut him off from the other shore which he is rapidly approaching, or of trusting to my Winchester before he lands.

I prefer the latter course, and with my wind somewhat recovered, and my breathing and pulse a little more regular—fire again.

A leap—a splash—and the head and antlers disappear.

Down goes the gun, and out go the oars. Another effort is necessary, for if the deer has not reached his blue coat, he may sink—but no—there he is—afloat, and now I can take it easy.

Hand over hand, still gasping for breath, I come up to the deer, floating on his side, his head and shoulders partly submerged by the weight of his horns.

A fine pair of antlers, just out of the velvet, as white as snow, with four prongs on each horn, graceful and regular. His skin is beautifully blue and sleek and smooth as a new gown.

Upon examination I find, that both shots have hit him. The first on account of my unsteadiness, or the motion of the boat, pulled to one side, and was buried in his shoulder and must have maimed one leg. The second shot, struck him squarely in the back of the neck, at the base of the head, where I had aimed.

Hark! The dog is nearing shore, and will soon be there, and I must pick him up.

Before leaving the deer, I bury the blade of my hunting knife, at the juncture of the neck and body, to give the blood an outlet, then pull back to the point, where the buck jumped in.

A few moments and Major plunges through the brush, singing at the top of his voice.

I watch him for a few minutes, as arrived at the lake, he dashes madly along the bank, a hundred yards, in one direction, then back again to the lost scent, and off as far in the opposite direction and back, still finding no trace of further tracks.

Then suddenly realizing that the deer has taken to the water, and perhaps escaped him, he rushes to the water's edge, and raising his head, gives a prolonged howl.

Now he sees me, and at my whoop and call, plunges into the lake. I pick him up, dripping. I pat him and speak words of praise and acknowledgement to him, and even allow him to shake himself, and scatter water all over me at pleasure.

He knows perfectly well, now, what has happened, but is anxious to have his doubts set at rest as to the fate of the deer, and no amount of coaxing or wheedling, of kicking or of pounding, will induce him to lie down.

There he stands erect, with his forepaws, on the edge of the boat, his head pointed as high as he can get it, with outstretched neck, and elongated nose, turning in every direction, sniffing the air, for a trace of the hunt.

Soon we are back at the deer's side and now the trouble is to prevent the dog from jumping into the water, and to keep him away from the buck long enough, to permit me, to slip a rope around the antlers, which I carry over the stern, and make fast.

Then we start for the island. Any one who has never tried it can form no idea of the tediousness, and labor involved, in towing a heavy body like a deer, partially submerged, behind a row boat. The greatest effort at the oars, only forces the boat forward, until the rope is taut, then the resisting body, seems to pull it back again all the way.

Progress, then is very slow, but the spoils being safe, time is no object. Arrived at the island and selecting a shelving spot, I land with Major, and drag up the deer as best I can, carefully guarding the antlers.

Major is almost beside himself, with joy, and alternately licks the deer's smooth side or laps the blood.

Soon the welcome crack of a gun is heard on the main shore, and I row over to fetch my guide. We return, dress the deer, get him, into the boat, and merrily return to camp.

Sport has not come back to his starter, so we hope, that our party at Catlin Lake, may have him, and his deer. The frequent shooting in that direction during the day, and their lateness in returning, all point that way.

And so it proves—they return to camp with a fine doe—tired out but happy.

A good day's hunt surely, and its details are recounted by each one of us over and over again, by the light of the camp fire.

Vension steak for supper—it is still fresh—but nothing else will satisfy us to-night.

"Cut out the tenderloin for us—broil it with bacon, and have it brown and juicy; open the can of currant-jelly—and by the way, boys, we must drink to our buck." Glasses are filled, and my guide toasts, "Here's to you, and wishing you ten years of life for every prong on his horns."—

The following morning we hold a council of war. It is still cloudy, and we have had enough hunting. It will take almost a whole day to tote the venison across the carries, so the boys propose that they commence carrying it out to-day, as we have signified our intention of returning home next day.

MY ADIRONDACK PIPE.

We are agreed; so they start off with the boat loaded with venison, and leave us to our own resources. We smoke a pipe, and prepare our rods, and by eleven o'clock, the wind having freshened, the clouds have all cleared, and it is a bright sunshiny day.

Having determined to try the pond with our rods, we row out of our sheltered bay. The wind is blowing hard across the lake, making a big swell, and many of the places I tried on the previous occasion, are too rough for fishing, So we row up between the islands, and selecting an old trunk that has fallen far out into the lake, we hold fast, and cast our lines.

In a few hours, we have half a dozen fine perch, weighing from one pound to a pound and a quarter, beside many smaller fish. They are all gamey and give us lots of sport, and we both enjoy these four hours as much as any during the trip. It is hard for us to make up our minds to stop, but being now three o'clock, and long past lunch hour, we turn campward.

In the woods, one cannot always be particular, either about the lunch hour, or the lunch itself, and we often go with only a piece of bread and cold meat or a lump of maple sugar.

Arrived at camp, we string the fish, and they are a pretty sight; then we fall to getting our meal.

Being an old woodsman, I take as much pleasure in cooking, as in eating a meal.

We build our fire, cut a steak out of the quarter, the guides left in camp, cut it up, dress it, and with two or three clean slices of bacon, set it broiling.

The water is put on for coffee, potatoes cleaned and put to boil, and with bread and butter, currant jelly, some canned vegetables— and later, preserves—not forgetting the attendant hearty appetites, we have a capital meal.

The boys get back, late in the afternoon, tired out, their clothes drenched from walking through the wet woods.

It always seems to me, that one gets a worse soaking in the woods after a heavy rain is over, than in the midst of the severest down-pour.

It is only after a storm is over that every tree and bush, every shrub and blade of grass seems to be water logged, and to deposit all its accumulated moisture on your garments as though nature provided you for that purpose.

Partly in the hope of adding to our

string of fish, and partly to be on the lake at sundown, I slip my rod into the boat, and pull across the lake again toward the islands.

Whether it is that I have not hit upon good places, or whether my heart is not in the work, I know not, but try as I will, I cannot get a bite. For half an hour or more, I pull from place to place, whipping the lake's surface, but with no success.

Finally disgusted, and seeing the sun is setting, I reel in my line, and depositing my rod carefully on the thwarts, throw myself into the bottom of the boat—face upwards—to watch the lovely changes going on about me.

The silence and the solitude are delicious. The wind, so unruly all day, has died down to a zephyr, which daintily ripples the lake, and makes miniature waves, that murmur against the boat's side. There is only a wafer-like plank between my ear and the water, otherwise even *its* faint language, as it frets under the boat's keel and swelling sides, would be inaudible.

In the west, where fortunately for me, there is a wide gap in the wall-like mountains, through which the outlet winds along Mt. Everet's base—a broad belt of deep and deepening orange is visible, encircling the earth. Above it hangs a long, narrow bank of dark steel clouds, contrasting sharply again, with the zone of bright white light that surmounts it. Higher up this merges into the soft blue of the sky, which in turn overhead, and on to the east, blends through tender tints of rose leaf and pink, into the poppy hue of those fiery cloud banks, riding in the distance over Santanoni

Right above my upturned face, in a blue field, like the mighty aureole of some god or goddess, radiating bars of red light hang quivering and pulsating in the air. They seem to have solid shape, and yet the eye feels, rather than sees, a wave like motion, swaying and running through them.

Bright and lurid they flare—then, while I gaze—they grow fainter and fainter—until they are gone, and the sky is as blue, where they late appeared, as all about.

The rosy hues are all growing dimmer; the white zone is fading into the blue; the dark steel clouds, have risen higher above the horizon, and in the higher light are white as a snowdrift; the orange belt is growing paler—

but oh, how brilliant and radiant and lovely!

'Tis changing still. The last traces of the wind have disappeared, and the glassy surface of the lake reflects only a soft, grey, colorless sky, with a brilliant white light in the western gap, as though at the closing of the gates of Paradise, one had been forgotten.

In the east the huge grim shadow of Santanoni, is gradually creeping over the waters, and night in her loveliest form and in her softest mood, wearing her jewelled crown, wings high over his crest.

But a minute ago and I could have counted the stars, now they are numberless—our earth is a mystery, full of mysteries; here are a million such.

It is a time and place to recall the most cherished memories, and inspire the highest thoughts, thrill the soul, like the harmonious strings of a harp, and attune it to worship!

A faint "Hilloa"! I raise myself, leaning upon my elbow, and looking out over the dark waters of the lake, see the bright flame and ascending column of smoke from our camp fire in the distance. It looks to be in the heart of the forest, and nowhere else do the trees seem so tall, so gaunt and weird.

Another "Hilloa"—and it only needs the sound of my answering whoop, to break the spell that has bound me.

* * * * *

It has been our habit to leave the flaps of the tent open at night, to admit the radiating heat, of the great fire, that we build every evening.

In the middle of the night, I suddenly awake, cold and shivering. The fire is almost out, there are only a few glowing embers, and the night has grown very cold. I prop myself on one hand, and gaze at my companions, slumbering peacefully, only their hats visible above the edge of the blankets. I cannot make up my mind to wake any of them, to renew the fire, so I slip noiselessly out of my blanket bag, and step without the tent.

It is a beautiful clear night, the myriad stars are sparkling with peculiar fire in the frosty air, the peaceful moon pours down her loving light, a message of rest and contentment, piercing through the envious foliage above, and tracing upon the ground, wavering patterns of exquisite beauty and delicacy.

But the cold recalls me. I stir the few remaining embers, and shaking them together, cover them with bark and small pine wood, over these throw a log or two, and soon the fire is snapping and blazing again.

Being wide awake, with little inclination to sleep, I light my pipe and sit down by the fire.

Major lies extended, where he can catch the most heat, his hind legs curled under him, his fore feet stretched out, and his nose resting on his paws. He is evidently agitated about something, and makes a sound like a suppressed bark, while his whole body quivers and trembles. He is dreaming.

He is after a big buck. Now his bark comes quick and short, as the scent is good, and the pace fast; suddenly he stops altogether—he has struck water, a brook or creek, and is hunting up and down for the scent—there, he has found it, and is off again, faster and faster; until he quickly leaps upon his prey, and the hunt is over. That is dog's Paradise.

Hoo-hoo—hoo-ooh! Hoo-hoo—hoo-ooh! there's an owl! listen a minute and the hoot will be repeated, or perhaps answered in the distance. I wonder, what this particular fellow, is so noisy about. Whether he is calling his mate? or whether he has just succeeded in securing a succulent rat supper, or is he playing at hide-and-seek with some of his jolly mates?

There's a loon's cry! Any one unfamiliar with it, hearing it at night, would think, the devil himself were let loose; or at least that a maniac were wandering around the lake shore.

I remember once, after breaking camp on Little Tupper Lake, my guide and I were rowing down the lake, through a heavy morning mist, which hung low upon the water's surface, completely hiding even the nearest objects from view. We had laid our course by the compass, and were rowing along, feeling our way carefully, when suddenly we were startled, by a most terrific and blood curdling shriek, right under our bow—a splash, and then all was still.

I stared at my guide in speechless horror, but he burst out laughing, and explained, that a loon must have risen to the surface close to the boat as we were approaching, and in the heavy mist was probably, almost run down, before he became aware of us.

A drowning human being could not have screamed in more agonizing tones.

There's the sharp barking of a fox! How I wish one would visit us, at camp. I should like a good fox rug—though I suppose, their fur would not be very thick or good now.

How harmless all these noises of the night appear, robbed of their terror by familiarity—they are even companionable.

But my pipe has gone out—I replace it in its case with a snap—take a drink of cold spring water, and with another look at the jewel-vaulted canopy overhead—slip back to my corner in the tent, having first carefully tied down the tent flaps.

* * * * *

We rise at daybreak and make an early breakfast. While the boys are cleaning and stowing the dishes and camp kit in the baskets, we pack our small valise, and strap our shawls and blankets. The fish are carefully packed, in layers of fresh green moss, at the top of one of the packs.

Then sorrowfully we pull down and roll up our little tent, disclosing the square patch, well covered with balsam boughs, where for a week, our party of four have lain side by side.

On one of the prominent trees near camp, we had fastened a single buckhorn, found near the spring by one of the guides ; and after it, we had named our camp. Under this emblem, we now make a broad blaze, and on it inscribe the names of our party, the dates of our arrival and departure, and the de-details of our success with rod and gun.

Tent, packs, bags and bundles—rifles and rods are now stored in our boats, and with the greatest regret we say farewell to Camp Buckhorn, where we had passed such a pleasant and successful week.

Through the lake with many backward glances at our beloved mountains, through the slang and over the carry, now thickly strewn, with a carpet of many hued leaves.

Arrived at the end of the carry we take up our venison, sent out the day before, then, pulling slowly up the lake against the usual headwind, we are home before evening, where many friends await us, to admire our trophies, prominently displayed on our boatload, to congratulate us on our success, and to assure us that they will gladly share in our fish and venison.

May we all meet again, in the Adirondack woods next year—I shall be there for one.

October, 1887.

www.ingramcontent.com/pod-product-compliance
Lightning Source LLC
Chambersburg PA
CBHW020325090426
42735CB00009B/1413